Creating
Print On Demand
Interiors & Covers
Using
Scribus 1.4.1

by

D. J. Mills

Tift Publishing

Creating Print on Demand Interiors & Covers Using Scribus 1.4.1

Published 2013 by Tift Publishing
www.tiftpublishing.com
Book and Cover design copyright © 2013 by Tift Publishing

ISBN-13: 9781393479895

Acknowledgements

My thanks and gratitude to my first readers
who helped to locate all the errors
I placed in the first draft.

Creating
Print On Demand
Interiors & Covers
Using
Scribus 1.4.1

by

D. J. Mills

Table of Contents

Creating POD Interiors using Scribus

What is Scribus?

Scribus is open source software that works similar to InDesign.

Scribus imports formatted text saved as .ODT, .HTML, and .CSV files. If you use LibreOffice or OpenOffice to create an .ODT file extension, your formatting will be imported to Scribus along with the text.

However, if you use Microsoft Word, or other text programs, Microsoft documents (.DOC) files and (.TXT) text files will import without formatting. This means you will do all your formatting inside Scribus. This is not a problem because I do format the text after it is imported into Scribus.

You can also copy the text from the program where you created the novel and paste it into the Scribus text frames, and once the text is formatted, Scribus exports to a PDF file.

You do not need to purchase this book to learn Scribus. You can go to the below link and work your way through the Help topics at your own pace to create interiors and covers for Print On Demand books.

There is much more to learn than required to produce novel interiors. You can produce newspaper column documents. You can produce PDF forms for your web site. You can produce business cards and many other layouts.

I have read all the Scribus help files to learn how the program worked with text such as tagged files, filtering imported text, text frame, styles, creating PDF forms, master pages with bleed areas, margins set, pagination, leading, tracking, kerning, inserting photos or images, headlines, and much more in the Scribus Open Source Desktop Publishing Help documentation at wiki.scribus.net under canvas/Help:TOC

I will cover the areas in Scribus that are the same as InDesign that I was taught to produce both interiors and covers for my novels.

Installing Scribus

To install Scribus you go to the Scribus site at www.scribus.net under canvas/Scribus and click the Download link. Select the download files link relating to your computer and operating system and follow their instructions in Installation, located in the left menu list on the Scribus site.

I installed Scribus version 1.4.1 with no trouble installing or using, except for the few anomalies adding pages and losing text frames, as mentioned later in this manual.

Scribus Help Documents

Scribus Help Documents have many other tools you can use in your layout of books, including columns for newsletters, tables for non fiction books, lists, and PDF Form Authoring (web forms).

You can learn how to set up **Table of Contents and Indexes, Hyphenation**, adding extra **Font families**, or **External Tools** in **File => Preferences** window.

Why use Scribus?

I wanted to make my Print On Demand Fiction books have the same professional look as traditionally published books, and from what I understand, they mostly use InDesign for the layout of the interiors. This is an expensive product. Even paying monthly for the privilege of using InDesign for just the month to get the next novel up on

CreateSpace is too expensive for some of us. Scribus does everything that InDesign does without the cost.

I write in Microsoft Word, edit, spell check and send the Word document to my beta readers. Once I receive their comments and make any necessary changes, I save a copy of the Word document for Smashwords ebook format, another copy to convert to HTML for Amazon ebook format, and a PDF for my files.

Using Scribus, I import the Word document and adjust the formatting, including tracking and kerning adjustments.

In the past, I went through the interior layout process for POD importing the whole file which includes forcing the new chapter text onto the next linked page by raising the bottom of the text frame on the last page of each chapter. Once I had each new chapter start on a new page, I set up styles, checked kerning and tracking, and all the other minor adjustments needed to improve the interior layout.

I realised that each time I altered the tracking to move a single word back onto the previous line of text, the following text also moved back a line. I had to readjust the bottom of the last text frame for each chapter to force the next chapter onto the next page again. Repetitive work but needed to get a professional finish to each page.

Now I import, or copy and paste, one chapter at a time, instead of the whole book into Scribus.

This is for ease of adjustments to tracking and kerning changes to paragraphs, without the need to unlink text boxes when inserting more pages or readjusting the start of the following chapters.

You may find importing the whole file easier and unlink to insert different template pages and relink for the text to flow as you make changes. You could also decide to write the story inside the text boxes in Scribus. I prefer to write in Word because I tend to use spelling checker a lot, and there are other tools in Word I created to check on overuse of words, read the text to me, etc.

Remember, if you use a different text program to Word, you can still follow the process to format your imported text in Scribus.

What I Will Not Cover

This book is a guide to use Scribus to layout your print book, but I will not teach which fonts to chose for headings or content in different genre books. I will not cover why you should remove widows and orphans. I will not cover what images to use on covers or in the interior of your books. or a host of other publishing guidelines.

You can learn more details on print layout by taking courses or spending time studying the fiction book layouts in your chosen genre or searching the internet for free information.

I will recommend two six week online courses I took that were well worth the small cost. They are Book Cover Design and Interior Book Design created by Dean Wesley Smith at deanwesleysmith.com under Online Workshops. I came away from the courses confident I could produce professional covers and interior layouts.

Both courses used InDesign costing U.S. $45.00 a month sub-scription, if you don't want to pay the full price for the program. You may also need to spend more money for tutorials on using InDesign at a site called Lynda.com for around U.S. $25.00 a month. The cost of both InDesign and Lynda.com was the main reason I learnt all I could about using Scribus.

Onward.

CreateSpace Requirements

You can read CreateSpace basic requirements for layout of your Covers and Interiors at https://www.createspace.com/Products/Book/

The main points needed are CreateSpace requires a print ready pdf file with fonts embedded to process for a Print On Demand (POD) book . The maximum accepted file size for the book interior is 400 MB.

The next important area of information is knowing the requirements for creating the interior PDF.

There are terms you may be unfamiliar with, but you need to learn them to understand the measurements required to set up a template for the interior.

Trim area
Where the page will be cut.

Bleed area
To print at or off the very edge of a page by design. Commonly used to accommodate images and illustrations.

Spine
The part of the cover that wraps around the bound edge of the book.

Gutter margins
These are the inside margins next to the book's binding. You'll want a wider margin for longer (thicker) books. See the table for setting your inside margins.

The below list is the correct measurements at the time of writing this, but you can check for changes on www.createspace.com under Products/Book/InteriorPDF.jsp.

Page Count	Inside (Gutter) Margins	Outside Margins
24-150 pages	.375"	At least .25"
151-400 pages	.75"	At least .25"
401-600 pages	.875"	At least .25"
More than 600 pages	1.0"	At least .25"

Outside margin

These are the page edges opposite the binding, and the top and bottom margins. All live text and images must have an outside margin of at least .25" -- but recommend an outside margin of at least .5".

Live Elements

The content within the viewable area (or safe zone) which is always seen. No essential elements are cut during the bookmaking process.

Expanded Distribution

To qualify for Expanded Distribution you have to either have your own ISBN or a CreateSpace assigned ISBN.

If you are using cream paper you have to use one of the following trim sizes to qualify for Expanded Distribution

Trim Sizes: 5" x 8", 5.25" x 8", 5.5" x 8.5" or 6" x 9"

Requirements before building templates

Size of book

The first requirement needed to create templates in Scribus is the Trim size of the book. CreateSpace lists the Trim sizes available for Black and White and Full Colour books at www.createspace.com in the /Products/Book/#content4 page.

Also needed are the number of pages to select gutter margin measurement, for both Black and White or Full Colour interiors.

Once the interior is formatted, the final page count is needed that includes front and back matter to calculate the spine of the cover.

I open my Word document, select all text, then set the page spacing to 1.5 and take a note of the number of pages.

My Example:
My example will be a 6" x 9" Black and White book with 152 pages. I need to include Front Matter (approximately 8 pages) and Back Matter (About the Author, Sample of next book, and list of available books and any links so another 8 - 10 pages) totalling 170 pages, so the Gutter Margin will be at least .75". I want the outside margin to be .5".

I also want to have headers and footers in the chapter pages, so I adjust the top margin to .82" and the bottom margin to .75".

Exercise:

Prepare your text to calculate page count.
1. Make a copy of your original draft and call it Scribus Your Title Name.doc or another recognisable name. You use this copy to make changes ready to import into Scribus.
2. Open the Scribus copy document in Microsoft Word.
3. Select all the text in your Word document.
4. Click on Format menu item, select **Paragraphs**.
5. The Paragraph window will open.
6. The first tab is **Indents and Spacing**.
7. Locate **Spacing**, click on the **Line Spacing** drop down list and select **1.5 lines**.

If you haven't already set up First Line Indent for paragraphs, do so now while all the text is selected and the Paragraph window is open.
1. Locate **Indentation**, click on the **Special** drop down list and select **First Line**.

2. In the **By** drop down list select or type in **0.5**.
3. Close the Paragraphs window, and save your text.

Look at the number of pages now the format is changed, and take note. That is the number you require to work out the gutter margins.
1. Enter the page count in the table below.
2. If you have not already done so, enter the book size you required in the table below.

Remember to use one of the book sizes listed in Expanded Distribution so your books will automatically be included in the book lists distributed to bricks and mortar book stores.

If the following is not included in your document, add extra pages for your Front Matter (I add 10) and Back Matter (I add 5). Remember, you can add or delete extra pages later.
1. Enter the updated total page count in the table below.

Next, go back to the Gutter Margins section above and work out your **Gutter Margin** measurement, and your **Outside Margins**.
1. Enter the Gutter Margin and Outside Margin measurement in the table below.

Now look at other books in your genre to get an idea of the size of the top and bottom margins.
1. Enter your top and bottom margins in the table below. You will create the template layout for the book, using the measurements in this table.

Book Size   ....
Number of Pages   ....
Gutter margins   ....
Outside Margins   ....
Top Margins   ....
Bottom Margins   ....

Scribus

The Main Window

The basics of Scribus is to set up Master Pages (document templates) that include text frames, paragraph styles and text filters, image frames and much more that give a consistent look to imported text.

Once the Master Pages are set up, they can be imported into other documents from within the current document.

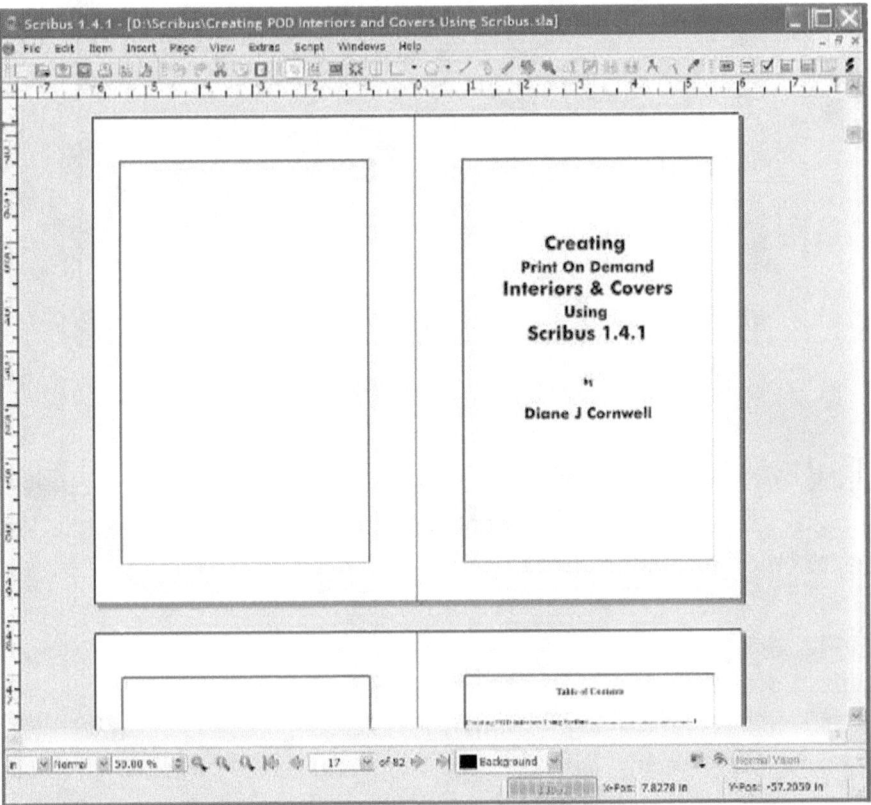

Create a new document

If you haven't done so already, locate the **Scribus** icon and double click to open, or locate Scribus in your **Start => Programs** list to launch Scribus.

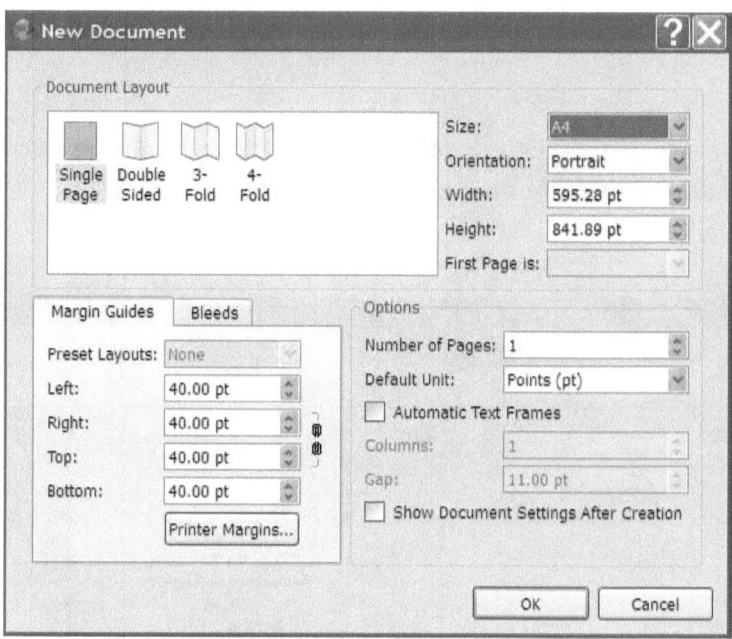

Click on the menu **File => New** to open the **New Document** window if the New Document window did not open when you started the Scribus program.

First, I set the **Default Unit** to Inches (in). If you work in centimetres or millimetres or points, set them first.

I select the **Double Sided Page** icon and set the width (6") and height (9") for my page size.

Recap: for a Novel size of 6 x 9 Inches I need:

6 x 9" Size	Margins	Text Boxes
Top	.82"	Header .3" by page width
Bottom	.75"	Footer .25" by page width
Inside	.875"	
Outside	.5"	

I set the **Inside Margin** to .875" and the **Outside Margin** to .5".

I set the **Top Margin** to .82" and **Bottom Margin** to .75".

First page is set to **Right Page** for novels.

Also note that the last page of your novel is always Left. If you finish your layout and realise it ends on the right hand side, then just add another blank page on the left.

Next I check the box for **Automatic Text Frame** and set **Columns** to 1 and **Gap** to 0. Think of using one column or two columns as in many non fiction manuals. In this case I only want one column (text box) per page.

I don't need to check the box **Show Document Settings after Creation**, because I can open the settings from the menu at any time by clicking File => Document Setup.

I can select 1 page or more than 1 pages. I select 3 pages so when the pages are displayed I can check whether the inner and outer margins are correct.

Once I confirm the settings are correct I click OK. The New Document window closes and 3 pages are displayed in the main area below the menus and short cut icons.

What I now have is three pages with one text box set within the margins selected in the New Document window. The first page is on the right, and the next two pages display side by side.

These are the pages required for the front matter and the back matter.

Exercise:

Create a new document by clicking on **File => New**.

1. Select **Double Sided** icon.
2. Set your **Default** unit.
3. Set your book size in **Width** and **Height**.
4. Set **Number of Pages** to 3.
5. Check the box for **Automatic Text Frame**.
6. Set **Columns** to 1 and **Gap** to 0.
7. Leave **Size** as Custom, and **Orientation** as Portrait.
8. Set your **Margin Guides** as per your calculations and CreateSpace recommendations.
9. Click **OK** button.
10. Confirm 3 pages are displaying in the main area, and the pages start on the right hand side.

You do not need to set **Bleeds** for interiors unless you are adding photos or images and you plan on them extending over the margins.

Master Pages

Now I want to make a template of the layout on the right Start Chapter pages, and the Left and Right Chapter pages.

Click on the menu item **Edit => Master Pages**.

The **Edit Master Pages** window opens. There are 4 icons across the top: Add a new master page, Duplicate the selected master page, Import master pages from another document and Delete the selected master page.

Below the four icons, the **Normal Left** and **Normal Right** template pages are already listed. These will be used for both Front Matter and End Matter pages. I will also use the Normal Left for the blank Chapter Start Left page, because it does not have a header or footer.

I need to add the other required pages: a **Right Chapter Start** page without header or footer, and a **Left** and **Right Normal Chapter** page with header and footer. If you decide to add a page number to the **Right Chapter Start** page, then you can add a footer to the template.

I set up the page numbers after I have the templates completed and added to the document.

Add New Template

Click the first icon, **Add a new master page**, type in the name of the new template and make sure the **Right Page** is selected then click **OK**.

The master page is displayed beside the **Edit Master Page** window and is already selected. If it does not display a red border, then click on the page and the border will change to red.

Copy a Template

An easy way to create a new template is to copy the Normal Left or Normal Right template then add extra text frames.

Click the second icon, **Duplicate the selected master page**. **Double click** the new master, named Copy #1 of Normal Left, if you had Normal Left selected before clicking on the Duplicate icon. The Rename Master window opens. Type in the new name for your master and click OK.

Import Master Pages from another Document

Click the third icon, **Import Master Pages from another Document**, and a new window will open called Import Master Page.

Click the **Select** button, and locate the document already created in your computer where the Master Page is located, and click **OK**. The window will close. Select the template you wish to import from the Import Master Page drop down list, and click Import.

Repeat for any other templates you wish to import into your document from other documents.

Delete a Master

Select the Master page from the list in Edit Master Pages window, and click the fourth button, **Delete the Selected master page**, and the selected master is removed from the list of Master pages.

Adding Header and Footer to the Template

Select one of the master pages in the Edit Master Pages list. It will display in the Scribus main window. You can now add other text frames to the page.

To add a footer to the selected page, click **Insert => Insert Text Frame**. Or click on the **Insert Text Frame** icon.

The mouse pointer will change to the Insert Text Frame icon. Move the mouse to the page where you want the Footer text box to start and hold down the left mouse button while dragging the mouse pointer across the page to where you want the footer text box to end and release the left mouse button.

You can adjust the height and width of the new text box by selecting the box, then Right click in the text box and select the **Properties** item from the drop down menu list. The Properties window will open and you can change the width and height of the text box.

To locate the exact width and height of the text frame in the normal left or normal right master, close the Master Page window. This brings you back to the main Scribus window, displaying the pages you created earlier.

Click on the text box in the right page, and the text frame will change to red. Right click inside the text frame and select **Properties** from the drop down menu list.

The properties window opens, showing the X and Y positions of the text frame, and the Width and Height. Take a note of these measurements, and close the Properties box. Now select the header or footer text frame, right click and select **Properties**. The properties window will open for the selected frame, and you can type in the width and height you require to align the header or footer. Close the Properties window, and check the frame moved to the correct position on the page.

You can also use the left and right arrows to move the text boxes to the correct position once the text box is selected, or use the X and Y position fields in the Properties window.

Repeat the above steps to create the template for the Normal Left Chapter Page and Normal Right Chapter Page, adding both a header and Footer.

Exercise:

Add a new master page.

1. **Edit => Master Pages**.
2. **Click** on the **New** Icon.
3. Name the new master page.
4. Select **Left** or **Right** for the page position in the drop down menu.
5. Add your required text boxes in the new blank master page.

Copy a master page.

1. Select the **normal left** master page.
2. Click the second icon, **Duplicate the selected master page**.
3. Double click the new master, named Copy #1 of Normal Left.
4. The **Rename Master** window opens.
5. Type in the new name for your master and click OK.

Delete a master page.

1. Select the new master page you created by copying the Normal Left master.
2. Click the fourth button, **Delete the Selected master page**.
3. The selected master page disappears from the list.

Create your Normal Chapter Left and Normal Chapter Right templates.

1. Select your normal left template.
2. Click the second icon, **Duplicate the selected master page**.
3. Double click the new master, named Copy #1 of Normal Left.

4. The **Rename Master** window opens.

5. Type in the Normal Chapter Left.

6. The new Normal Chapter Left template should show in the list of templates.

7. Add the header and footer boxes to the template.

8. **Insert => Insert Text Frame** and place the header box and adjust as necessary either by dragging the edges of the box or by right clicking in the selected box and selecting **Properties** menu item.

9. Repeat for the footer.

10. We will add text to the header and footer in the next exercise.

11. Repeat these steps to create your Normal Chapter Right template.

Story Editor

Once the text boxes are in place on the new templates, right click in the Left Normal Chapter page header text box and select Edit Text from the drop down menu list.

The Story Editor will open. Here is where you do all your formatting of your text, including Paragraph Styles, Font Selection, Font Sizing, Tracking and Kerning.

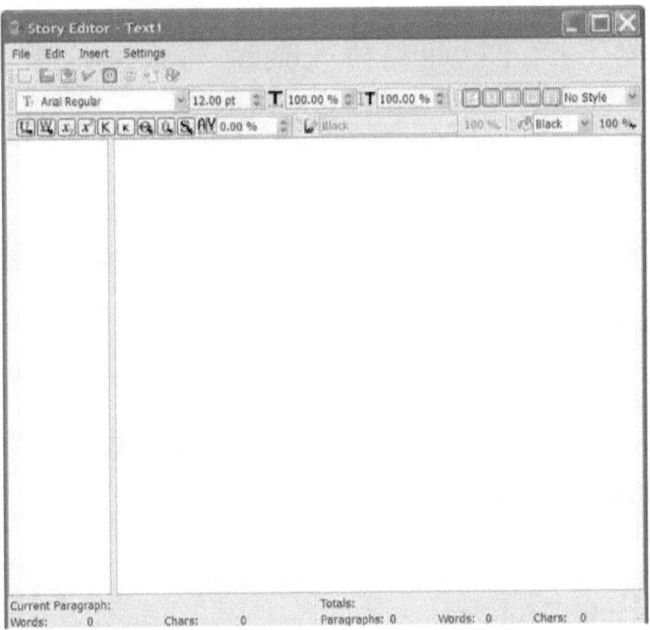

For now I select the Left Header and type in "Author Name", centre it and click the green check icon to save the text in the template. The Story Editor closes.

In the Right Normal Chapter Header I type "Book Title", centre it, then click the green check icon to save the text in the template. The Story Editor closes.

In the Story Editor for both the Left and Right Footers, I click **Insert => Character => Page Number**.

A "#" sign appears in the footers. I centre the page marker for both left and right footers. You may left justify the left page, and right justify the right page, if you wish. Click the green check icon to save the text in the template. The Story Editor closes.

Note: The actual page numbers will be configured later under **File => Document Setup => Sections**.

My template list now displays Normal Left, Normal Right, Chapter Start Right Page, Normal Left Chapter Page and Normal Right Chapter Page.

I close the Edit Master Pages window.

I am now ready to insert pages as needed when I import my document.

Exercise:

1. Open your master pages window in Scribus.
2. Select your Normal Chapter Left template.
3. Select the header box.
4. Right click inside the selected box and click on Edit Text menu item to open the Story Editor.
5. Type "Author Name" in the text area.
6. Justify the text.
7. Select the text and change the font and size.
8. Click **File => Update Text Frame and Exit** or click the update icon (fourth icon from left) or use the short cut keys Ctrl+W.
9. Select the footer text box and open the Story Editor.
10. Click **Insert => Character => Page Number**.
11. Justify and select font and font size.

12. Save the changes.

13. Open your Normal Chapter Right template.

14. This time add the text "Title of your Book" in the header text area, justify, select font and size, and save.

15. Add the page number character in the footer.

16. These templates can now be used by importing into all your future Scribus projects.

17. Close your Edit Master Pages window.

Add Pages.

To add pages to the document, select the page where you want to add pages.

Click **Pages => Insert**. The Insert Page window opens.

Select the number of pages to insert and select either Before Page, After Page, or at End.

Select which templates you want to use, Normal Left and Normal Right, or other left or right template pages you created.

Make sure Move Objects with their Page is checked, then click OK.

Next you need to link the inserted pages to the pages before and after. If the pages are added in the wrong place, locate them, delete them by selecting the page, right click the mouse on the page and select Delete Page, then add the pages again in the correct place.

Linking pages

If adding pages at the end of the document, the link from text box to text box will automatically continue. However, if adding pages before or after a selected page, the link must be removed and linked to the inserted pages in the Item menu list or by using the icons.

To check the pages are linked select the text frame on the first page and click the Unlink Text Frames icon. The pages with links will display arrows showing the direction of links.

To link text frames, select the last linked text frame, click the Link Text Frames icon, then click the next page text frame you want the text to flow to.

To unlink, select the text frame on the page you want unlinked then click the Unlink Text Frames icon. Now select the previous page, the page you want to unlink.

To confirm the link was broken, click on the Link Text Frame icon and the arrows will display all the pages that are linked. There should not be an arrow between the two pages you selected.

Note: One problem I encountered was that the page just linked did not display the arrow showing the new link. I scroll the window of displayed pages up and down and the link displays as it comes back into view in the main work area.

To remove the displayed links, I click the Esc key on my keyboard and the links disappear.

I unlink the last page of the current chapter to the Chapter Start Right page of the next chapter.

Another way to see all the linked pages is to turn on linking by opening the Document Setup window and in **Display**, check **Display Text Chains** in the **General** tab. Click the **Apply** button and **OK** to close the Document Setup window.

Another problem I experienced when inserting pages Before or After the selected page, the new pages are added but the text boxes disappear. I scroll to the bottom of the main window below all the displayed pages to locate the text boxes, copy the box, then delete it, and move back up to the added page and paste the text box onto the page. If it is not aligned with the text frame outline, I move the text frame with the arrow keys on the keyboard so they line up with the text frame outline.

However, if I only add new pages to the end of each chapter, the problem of disappearing text frames does not happen. This may be an anomaly with my computer or a coding error in the Scribus program.

Delete Pages

I then delete any extra pages in the current chapter that do not have text by selected the page I want deleted. I make sure the red border of the selected page is displayed, then right click the mouse and select the last menu item, **Delete Page**.

The Delete Pages window opens. To delete one page, I confirm the page number in the **Delete From** and **to:** list and click **OK**. If I want to delete more than one page, I change the to: field to the number of pages I want deleted and click OK.

The pages are removed from the list of pages in the document.

Recap:
Set up a document to the size of the book you wish published.
Create templates that you will use in your document.
Add or delete pages from the document.
Link or unlink text frames so the text flows from page to page.

The templates I use are:

1. Normal Left and Normal Right for Front and Back Matter.
2. Chapter Left Start is the same as Normal Left, which I leave

blank if the previous chapter ended on a right page.

3. Chapter Right Start which does not have a header or footer.

4. Chapter Left Normal and Chapter Right Normal which both have a header for the Title of the book and the Author Name typed in, and both have a footer for the page number.

When I import the Chapter Left and Right Normal template into a new document, all I have to do is type the actual book title and author name in the template headers and as I add the template pages to the document the title and author name are already displayed.

Exercise:

Practice adding and deleting pages, both at the end and in the middle of other pages in the file.

1. Add pages to the front matter pages.
2. Add left chapter header page.
3. Add right chapter header page.
4. Add 2 or more left and right normal chapter pages.
5. Add 2 or more end matter pages.

Page Numbering Sections

Once the page number marker is in the master pages footers or headers, you nominate the sections where you want the page numbers to appear. This is set in the Sections area of the Document Setup window.

Click **File => Document Setup**, then scroll down to locate the **Sections** icon in the icon list on the left of the Document Setup window.

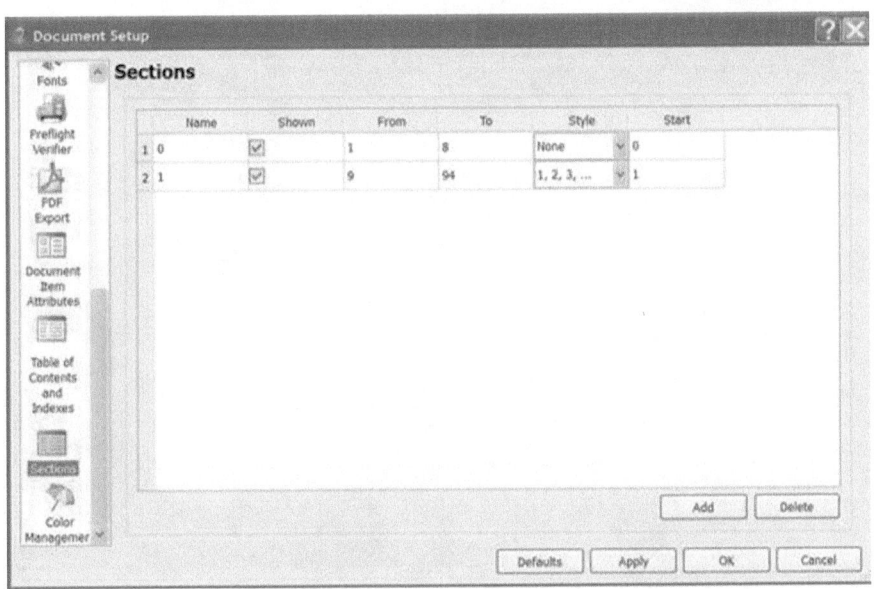

On the right, nominate the pages with no numbering, and the pages with numbering. I do not number the Front Matter so I select from 1 to 10 and set the **style** to **None**.

I start numbering from **page** 11 to total of novel pages and set the **style** to **1, 2, 3, . . .**

I make a third section for the Back Matter and select **None** for the **style**.

I click **Apply**, and close the window.

If I add more pages later, I check and adjust the **From** and **To** fields for each section.

Exercise:

1. Open the **Document Setup** window and in the **Sections** area set the page number areas and apply.
2. If you already have template pages with footers added to your file, confirm the page marker has changed to page numbers, if not, add some template pages with footers and confirm the page numbers are displayed.

Paragraph Styles

The main two paragraph styles I use are Indent for the story text and Centred for the chapter names and numbers. There are many others, such as Dropped Caps, Heading 1, Heading 2 and Heading 3 for non-fiction.

These paragraph styles are set up in **Edit => Styles** to open the Style Manager.

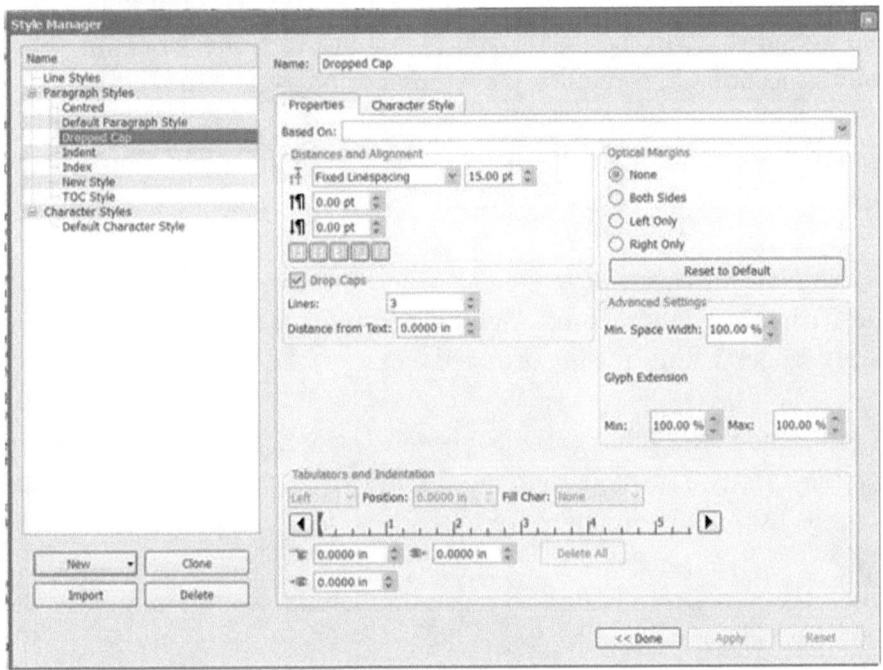

Click the **New** button, Select **Paragraph Styles** to display the **Properties** and **Character Style** tabs on the right hand side of the Styles Manager.

Enter the name **Indent**. Under the ruler at the bottom, enter the inches for the indent. I enter 0.3000. The Indent icon appears on the ruler. I leave all the other settings as default.

Under the Character Style tab I select **Times New Roman** family font and Regular Style. I select 12.00 pt for the size and leave the other settings as default then click the **Apply** button to save the settings.

I click the **New** button again to create the next paragraph style and name the paragraph style **Centred**. I click the **centred alignment** icon, second from the left in the 5 icons under Distances and Alignment.

Under the Character Style tab I select **Times New Roman** family font and **Regular** Style. I select 12.00 pt for the size and leave the other settings as default, then click the **Apply** button to save the settings.

Another Paragraph Style that is handy to have is **Dropped Caps** for the first letter of the first word for the first sentence of each new chapter.

Select **New Paragraph Style** and name it **Dropped Cap**. I click on the **Drop Caps check box**. A green check mark appears in the check box. I select **3 lines** for the dropped cap.

Again, under the **Character Style** tab I select **Times New Roman** for the family font and Regular for the style, leave the rest of the settings as default and click Apply.

Click the **< < Done** button to close the details section and close the Styles window.

I open the Story Editor to confirm the newly created styles are now available and test each paragraph style on some text to confirm my settings are correct.

I suggest you test the Drop Cap settings in the Story Editor and make changes as required to the number of lines to drop the capital letter and the distance from text measurement.

One more style that is useful is the Table of Contents style.

In the Style Manager, click **New Paragraph** Style button. Name the new paragraph style **TOC**. In the Properties Tab, I click the mouse pointer on the ruler at either 4" or 4.25". A tab symbol appears on the ruler. I move it left or right until I am happy with the placement of the tab. This is the spot that the page number will appear in the Table of Contents.

I select **Dot** from the drop down list for **Fill Char:** above the ruler. The space between the name in the TOC and the page number will be filled with a line of dots. I leave the left edge of the TOC listings at 0.0000 inches, but you can alter the left edge (margin) inwards if you wish.

I also change the **Fixed Linespacing** to 10.00 pt. This allows for more items to be displayed on the one page. If, once the TOC is generated and it goes over two pages, I can come back into the Style Manager and alter the Fixed Linespacing setting and regenerate the TOC so that all the contents are displayed on one page.

In the Character Style tab, I select Times New Roman for the font family, and Regular for the style. I change the size of the font to 10 points because I think that looks better in the generated Table of Contents.

The rest of the setup of the TOC is discussed later, after I import the text, format it and confirm each page is correctly laid out, with no widows or orphans. Only once I am happy with the finished product, do I select each topic heading or chapter heading that will be included in the TOC.

Exercise:

1. Create a paragraph style for indented paragraphs, centred, Dropped

Cap and TOC, and close the Styles Manager.

2. Right Click on the text box in your first page to open the Story Editor.

3. Click on the Styles drop down list to check the newly created paragraph styles are listed.

4. Type some paragraphs of text, highlight them, and click on the drop down style list to the left of the text and select the centred paragraph style. The typed text moves to the centre of the text area.

5. Select the first paragraph, click in the first word, and select the Drop Cap Style.

6. Save and close the Story Editor and confirm your text changed to you style settings on the displayed page in the main window.

Fonts

Font for Title and Author Name on Cover

Cover Fonts are usually a much larger size than interior fonts but are not necessarily the same fonts as used in the interior.

Font for minor text fields on Cover

The minor text fonts used on the cover can be carried into the interior layout and used for title, author name and chapter headings.

Study books in the genre you are working on, and select similar or the same font as the layout you like best in a published book.

Font for text

Header, footer, chapter titles and chapter text fonts can be selected via the **Story Editor** or set up in the **Document Setup** window.

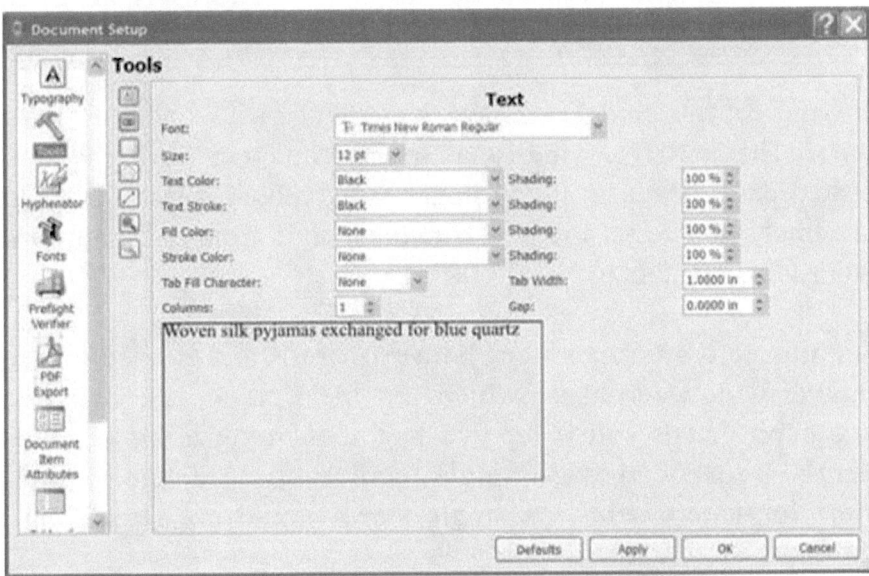

To set the text font in the **Document Setup** window, click on the **Tools** icon in the left column. Then make sure that the first icon in the second column of smaller icons is selected. The word Text will appear at the top of the list of fields.

Select the font from the drop down list of fonts and a sample of the font will display at the bottom of the window.

I set the size of the font to 12 pt. Remember, these settings can be changed once the text has been imported from the Story Editor.

I find it is easier to set the font here, then I only have to change the font for the chapter headings in the Story Editor after I import the text.

Font size, Leading, Tracking and Kerning

Once the text is imported, Leading, Kerning, Tracking and the font sizes are all altered in the Story Editor.

Leading is the space between the lines of text and will remain as 1.5 as set in the Word Document.

Remember, you can create new paragraph styles under **Edit =>** **Styles**. The new style will display in the drop down list in the Story Editor. Place the curser in the single paragraph, or select a group of paragraphs and select the new paragraph style from the drop down list inside Story Editor.

Kerning refers to the spaces between words and is used to help remove widows/orphans, which are the first or last line of a paragraph that is split over two pages. Kerning is also used to compress text to move a single word back up a line, because some formatters believe a single word should not remain on a line by itself.

I believe Kerning is the magic that removes white spaces in every page by adjusting the kerning 1-3 percent in each paragraph where needed to remove a single word from a line, or a single line of a paragraph from the bottom or top of pages.

In Story Editor, select the line or paragraph of text that needs adjusting and change the percentage of the **Manual Tracking** configuration (the T with the red horizontal arrow under the letters, next to font size) either plus or minus the percentage, for example -1%, then update the text frame and exit the Story Editor to check if the percentage change was enough to compress the spacing to roll the single word back to the previous line of text.

If not, go into the Story Editor again and repeat the steps until the single word moves back to the previous line.

I also look for any words that can be hyphenated to help close the spaces in the paragraph where any single word needs pulling back to the previous line.

Tracking is setting the individual letter spacing in a word.

In the Story Editor, select the word, then alter the **percentage** of the **Manual Tracking** configuration (the T with the red horizontal arrow under the letters) to close any gaps or expand the space between letters of the word.

Exercise:

1. Set your font and size for Title and Author Name in your header template by selecting the text frame and right clicking the mouse and selecting **Edit Text** to open the **Story Editor**.
2. Select the Title and set the font and font size.
3. Click the **Update Text Frame and Exit** icon or type **Ctrl+W** to save and close the Story Editor.

4. Set your font and size for Page Numbers in your chapter template footers. Save and close Story Editor.

5. Select your font for your text in the **Document Setup => Tools => Text** window. Click **Apply** button, and close the window.

The above steps may seem like a lot of work at first, but once you have the templates created, you can import them into every future novel layout.

The only changes you need to make in each new file are selecting different fonts for different genre books, adding hyphenation and altering the Tracking and Kerning to remove spaces.

Now you have a feel for all the configurations, you are ready to import the text.

Creating Interior of Book

Preparing Text in Word Document Before Importing

To save myself a lot of time reading through the text after I import into Scribus I always do one last check in my Word document before importing, because Word tools take a lot of the workload out of editing.

First I run a spell and grammar check to catch any mistakes added during editing of my story, and confirm line spacing is set to 1.5.

Spell Check

Word has a relatively good spell checker, so use it to check the spelling before importing.

Grammar Check

To activate the grammar portion of the spell check, make sure the Check grammar check box at the bottom of the Spelling and Grammar window is selected. The Options button allows for more configuration selections for grammar checking.

Line spacing

If you have not got your line spacing as 1.5 lines then make it 1.5 lines now.

Marking Italics

Because Scribus does not import Word Document formats with the text, I mark all the formatted text in Word before importing.

I do not use underlines or bold in my fiction text, but I do use italics for names of space ships, individual character thoughts, and for characters who mind speak to other characters.

To overcome the lack of automatically importing italics, I mark all my italic text by using **Find** italic font and **Replace** located text with **<i>italics font</i>**.

In case you are not familiar with the coding required to make this a simple task, the steps are:
1. In Word document open the **Find and Replace** window: **Edit =>** **Find** or **Ctrl+f**.
2. Place the curser in the **Find What:** field, and press **Ctrl+i** to make the format read **Font: Italic**.
3. In the Replace Tab, type **<i>^&</i>**.
4. Click the **Find** button.
5. The search will stop when it locates italics.
6. Click the **Replace** button to wrap the <i> and </i> around the italicised text.
7. Once you confirm the code is correct click the **Replace All** button and let the search program locate and edit all the italicised text.

Marking Paragraph Styles

Marking paragraph styles if using different styles throughout the book is easy because Scribus has the ability to read tags during importing and assigning different paragraph styles to the tags.

You can learn more about Marking Paragraphs in the Word document before importing into Scribus, by reading the Text Frame page, under the Tagged Files heading on the Scribus website at wiki.scribus.net in the canvas/Help:Manual_Textframes page.

However, I am happy to manually alter the chapter headings and scene breaks while checking correct chapter order and chapter length.

I also like to check each first paragraph drop capital to make sure the paragraph covers two to three lines if the Drop Capital is set to drop three lines. If there is only one line in the first paragraph, there is a gap before the next paragraph starts, and I fix it as I go by either making the first paragraph longer, or incorporating the second paragraph into the first paragraph.

Delete Any Front And Back Matter

If I am importing the whole document, I delete any front and back matter from the Word Document, because I prefer to import them separately to the main document, but if I am copying one chapter at a time, I leave the front and back matter in the document.

Once I confirm the Word document is formatted correctly I am then ready to import into Scribus.

Exercise:

First steps are for Word, Libre and other document file types.
1. If you have not already done so, make a copy of your draft document to use for importing into Scribus.
2. Run Spell Checker on your draft document copy.
3. If you have not already altered the text to 1.5 line spacing do it now.

For Word Document file types only:
4. If you use italics in your story, mark your italic text with the above Find and Replace steps.

Everyone:
5. Delete any front and back matter, or copy the text to another file for importing into the Scribus Front and Back Matter templates.
6. Save the document.

Extra note for importing from Word.

If you can open your Word.doc file in Libre or another document program that retains the formatting of the Word document, you can save the file with an .ODT file extension, and import that version of your text into Scribus. It will import all formatting along with the text, saving you the extra work of Step 4 above, and searching for your marked text to format again in Scribus.

It worked for me when I tested it. I will add that step to my future book layouts.

Importing Front Matter Text

Front Matter Template

In Scribus, I add 10 pages using the Normal Left and Right templates for my Front Matter including blank pages.

Must haves in the Front Matter are Title Page and Copyright Page, but you may include a list of other books in the same genre, a second Title Page including the publisher contact details, a Table of Contents, and Dedication and Acknowledgement pages if you use them.

The best way to work out which Front Matter pages you need is to study books in your genre, noting the order of the information and whether left or right pages are blank pages. The same goes for studying Back Matter as discussed below.

Inserting Front Matter

I copy and paste or type my Front Matter into Story Editor because I use the same text as for my ebooks and it is easy to open each file, select the text, copy, and paste into each Text Frame on each unlinked page in Scribus.

My order of Front Matter:
- Review Quotes or Pull (right)
- Blank (left)
- List of other books in same genre (right)
- Blank (left)
- Title Page with Publisher's Logo (right)
- Copyright (left)
- Dedication (right)
- Blank (left)
- Title Page (right)

If I included a Table of Contents, I would place it on a right hand page after the final title page, adding a blank left page before the TOC page. If I omit any Front Matter pages I also remove the corresponding blank page.

Formatting

I copy in the Pull text, select the text and pick the correct font from the drop down list, then alter the size, fully justify the text, and check Kerning and Tracking in case of spaces between the words.

I use Drop Capital for the first paragraph in Pull sample, and Indent style for the rest of the paragraphs, then make sure the text takes up less than half the page.

I confirm my list of other books is up-to-date and copy the list and paste into the third Front Matter page. I centre justify the list.

The same with the first Title Page, but I use the same font selected for the cover, and make it smaller and centre the text.

I left justify the copyright page, and make the text size smaller than the other pages in the Front Matter and leave a marker for adding the ISBN number after it is assigned by CreateSpace.

An example is: "ISBN: 13 digit number goes here"

After I receive my 13 digit ISBN number, I paste it into the allotted space on the Copyright page, making sure I delete any left over part of "13 digit number goes here", then recompile a PDF file in Scribus before uploading to CreateSpace.

I use italics for the Dedication font and the same text size as the copyright page.

The final title page is a copy of the first title page, but with the publisher information deleted. Same font, and same size.

Exercise:

1. If you have not already worked out your Front Matter order, do so now.
2. Open Scribus, and your POD file if not already open.
3. Add your front matter template pages from your Normal Left and Normal right templates.
4. Open Story Editor by selecting the text frame, right click mouse, and select **Edit Text** in the drop down menu.
5. Type your text in the Story Editor.
6. If you import your Front Matter text, select the text frame, right click mouse, and select **Get Text** in the drop down menu. You may need to adjust the bottom of some text frames upwards to force the text to flow to the next page and confirm the next page text frame is linked to the current page text frame.
7. If a **small red rectangle** with an **X** inside it appears in the right lower corner of the text frame, it means there is not enough space to display the imported text. You will need to insert another page, and confirm it is linked to the previous page for the text to flow across.
8. Select your text and set the paragraph styles, font and size and justification.
9. If you need to hyphenate any words to close white spaces in the text, do so.
10. Save your changes.

Importing Chapter Text

First, a recap on the different Chapter Templates.

Each chapter starts on the right hand side of the book, so if a chapter ends on the right hand side, I insert a blank left page next. This means no header or footer, just a blank page.

The only time I would start chapters on the left hand side is if the word count for the story is over 100,000 words and I wanted to keep the book spine from getting too wide. I would not have blank left pages. Instead I would start each new chapter on the next page, either left or right thereby cutting down the width of the spine.

My decision would also depend on the genre and how other publishers display each chapter start. I have noticed a lot of fantasy stories treat longer works this way. You decide based on the genre you write.

Chapter Blank Left
- No header
- No footer page number
- No text in text frame, or, create the template without a text frame

If the blank chapter start left side template has a text frame because I copied the normal left template and labelled it Chapter Start Left template, then I unlink from the previous page text frame so the text will not flow in the text frame on the blank page.

Then add a Chapter Start Right template.

Chapter Start Right
- No header
- Page number in footer or not, depending which you chose. I do not

have a page number in the footer on the Chapter Start Right template.
• Left, Centre or Right justified if the page number marker is inserted.
• Link the last chapter right page text frame to the chapter start right text frame.

Next, I add 4 or 6 pages, selecting Chapter Left and Chapter Right templates and let the text flow over the pages. I keep adding more chapter pages until the end of the chapter, and repeat the process of adding the next chapter start pages and unlinking from the left page and linking to the right page. The text will continue to flow.

Chapter Left
• Header Author Name, Left, Centre or Right justified
• Page number in footer justified, Left, Centre or Right justified

Chapter Right
• Header Title, Left, Centre or Right justified
• Page number in footer, Left, Centre or Right justified

Appending groups of pages to the file automatically links the text frames, but if I insert a different template before a selected page, I always check and correct the links.

I select the first Chapter Start Right text frame and click on Unlink Text Frames icon to double check the front matter is not linked. Once I confirm there is no link, I right click the mouse. I select Get Text from the drop down menu, enter the path and select the Word document file.

In **Importer:** field, I select Word Documents. I leave **Import Text Only** check box empty, then click the **OK** button.

The file loads in the text frame and flows into the linked pages. If there are only a few pages added to the file you will notice a small red box with a X in it at the bottom of the last page text frame,. This indicates more text to be displayed.

Add more pages by selecting the page displaying the red box, then click the menu item **Page => Insert** to add more pages after the selected page.

Repeat inserting more pages until the red box with the X disappears, indicating no more text to display.

If the start of the next chapter does not start on the next page, move the bottom of the text frame up until the new chapter header disappears. It will flow onto the next page.

I chose not to use this process. Instead, I open the Word document, and copy one chapter at a time and paste it into the Chapter Start Right page text frame, adding more chapter pages until the whole chapter of text is displayed.

I delete any extra blank pages, then add the next Chapter Start Left and Right pages, and enough Chapter Left and Right pages, and remove any links to the previous chapter before I copy and paste the next chapter into the Story Editor text area.

I repeat for all the chapters.

The main reason for copying the text in to the Story Editor is the ease of removing widows and orphans without moving the next chapter up or down the next page.

Formatting

I work through each chapter in the Story Editor formatting the text.

First, I select all the text and set the font and size, if not already set.

While the text is still selected I set the paragraph style.

Next, I select the chapter title and centre it.

I place the curser in the first paragraph and select Drop Down paragraph style.

I locate any scene breaks and centre them.

Then I use **Find** to locate the italics markers and change the text to italics. I also use Find to locate the <i> and delete. I repeat for </i>.

I work through every chapter until the text is correct.

After I close the Story Editor I scan the chapters, looking for single lines of paragraphs displayed at the start or end of every page, or the last word of a paragraph on a line by itself. If I locate any, I go into the Story Editor and select the paragraph and alter the tracking to move the word onto the previous line, by changing tracking from 100% down to 97% or up to 103%. Tracking is the T with the red line under it, next to the font size field.

If I can't track the change without it being obvious I compressed the spaces, I look at hyphenating words to help force the single word onto the previous line.

What I end up with is a professional layout of the chapters.

Remember, you can code the Word document text to automatically use paragraph styles, but coding does not work with character styles when importing Word documents.

Exercise:

1. Import your Word document into Scribus, either using **Get Text**

menu selection in the drop down list or by copying the chapters and paste into the Story Editor window.

2. Select the correct Font and size, paragraph styles and justify chapter headers and scene breaks if you use them.

3. Look for and remove any widows and orphans.

Importing Back Matter Text

Lastly, I add more Normal Left and Right template pages for the Back Matter, importing the text exactly the same as for the Front Matter.

My order of Back matter:
- Tease chapters of next story in series (start on the right page)
- Blank (left) if the tease chapters end on the right hand page
- About the Author and, if room, contact details for Author (right)
- Blank (left)
- List of other published books by author (right)
- Blank (left)

I work through each page, keeping the font and size consistent with the front matter and the tease chapters the same as the book chapter layout.

Exercise:

1. Import or copy your Back Matter into your Scribus file.
2. Format the text.

Page Numbering

Once I am happy with the formatting, I take a note of the page number the story starts and ends, then click **File => Document Setup** to open the **Document Setup** window.

I navigate to **Sections** and set up the page numbering, as discussed on page 25.

To recap, I leave **Name** as 0 but you can change it to Front Matter. I make sure **Shown** check box is checked, **From 1 To 10** and select **None** in **Style**.

I add the next section, called 1, but you can call it Story, make sure **Shown** check box is checked, enter 11 in From and 303 (the page you write The End after the last chapter) in To, and selected 1, 3, 3, . . . in Style. Start should display 1, but if not, click in the Start field for the second section and type 1.

I do not number the pages in the End Matter, so do not even enter the section. If you decide to enter the End Matter section, make sure you enter the correct page numbers in From and To, and select None in Style.

Exercise:

1. Enter the start and end page numbers in **Sections** in your **File => Document Setup** window.
2. Save and close the Document Setup window and confirm the page numbers are displayed in your footers.

Inserting Graphics

I noticed a few Science Fiction and Fantasy novels included graphics at the start of each chapter.

One book had a drawing of one of the characters in the novel at the start of each chapter. Another novel had items displayed and a third had scenery displayed at the start of each chapter.

If you want graphics in your novel, it is quite easy to include them.

Remember the blank left page at the start of each chapter? Well, you can display your black and white graphic there, simply by removing the text frame and adding a image frame in the same place.

It is important to remember to keep the graphic inside the margins that border the page. If you chose to make the graphic cover the margins then you have to treat the size of the page differently. This will be covered in the next section on creating covers in Scribus.

I love the idea of including graphics if I put together a collection of short stories that have covers already created for the ebooks. I would start each short story on the right side and include a black and white version of the ebook cover on the left side.

I can't wait to try that later. But for now I will get my novels and collections of novella and novelettes out first.

Exercise:

1. Open a new file in Scribus.
2. Add a few pages.
3. Import text to fill the text frames.
4. Remove the link from the text frame on the left page.

5. Link the previous text frame to the next page text frame. The text will flow onto the next text frame.

6. Place a image frame in the same area on the page where you removed the text frame.

7. Select **Insert => Insert Image Frame** and place the changed curser in the top left corner and while holding the left mouse button, drag the mouse down to the bottom right corner and release the mouse button.

8. You can right click on the frame and select **Properties** to alter the size of the image frame.

9. Right click the mouse in the frame and select **Get Image** from the drop down menu.

10. Navigate to the file and select it.

11. Right click the image and select **Adjust Image to Frame** to make the image fit the Image Frame.

12. Move the image around until you are satisfied with it, then right click the mouse in the image and select **Is Locked**, so you don't accidently move it later.

13. Save and close the file.

Generating Table of Contents

Your story is now laid out as any publisher would arrange it.

Once you are satisfied with the layout, you need to compile your Table of Contents. Usually, this will be the front matter, chapter titles for fiction, and back matter.

If you have not already inserted a Front Matter Page to list your TOC then do so now and take a note of the text frame number. Remember, click on the text box to select it, right click the mouse and select Properties to open the Properties window. The text box name is at the top of the Properties window. Close the Properties window.

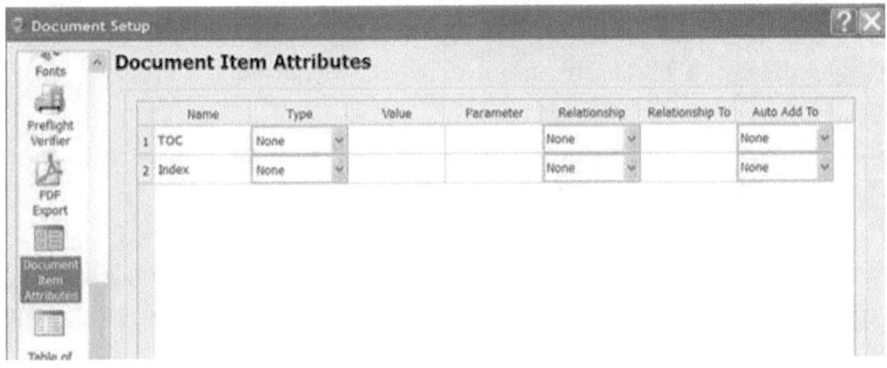

Click on **File => Document Setup** and locate the **Document Item Attributes** Icon in the left hand column. Click on it.

To create a new Document Attribute click on the **Add** button. Type TOC in the Name field and click the **Apply** button.

Next, click on the **Table of Contents and Indexes** Icon to open the properties section.

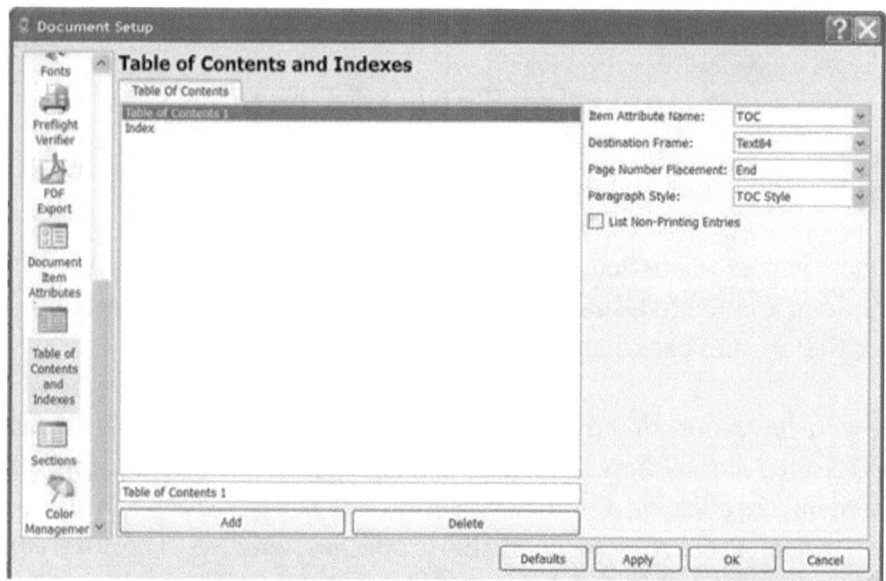

Click the **Add** button to add a new TOC. Type a different name in the field above the Add button, or leave the default of Table of Contents 1. Select TOC in the **Item Attribute Name** drop down list. This is the same TOC attribute you created first.

Select your text field number on the page you wish to display the TOC from the **Destination Frame** drop down list.

Select End from the **Page Number Placement** drop down list. This will place each page number at the end of each row in the generated TOC.

Select TOC Style in the **Paragraph Style** drop down list. This is the Paragraph Style you created earlier. Click the **Apply** button and then the **OK** button to close the Document Setup window.

Now the TOC is set up ready to add items.

I start on the first page of the interior layout pages, and select the text frame containing the text I want in the TOC. I right click the

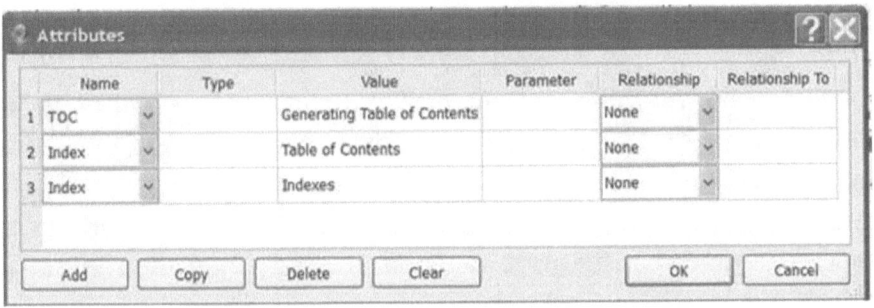

mouse in the text frame and select **Attributes** to open the Attributes window.

I click the **Add** button to add the first TOC element. I select TOC in the **Name** field, and type in the **Value** field the name I want displayed in the TOC. For this book's TOC I typed in Creating POD Interiors Using Scribus. I added a second TOC element for this book called What is Scribus. Click OK to close the Attributes window. These were the two headings on the page.

I scroll through the pages, selecting each page text field and enter the Attributes details for each TOC element. Once I have selected the text fields (pages) for all the elements I am ready to generate the TOC.

Important: Make sure no text frame is selected before you generate the TOC or you will find the TOC generated and displays on the selected text frame rather than the designated text frame.

I tend to select the text frame in the front matter where I want the TOC to display before I generate the TOC to make sure it displays in the correct page.

Click on **Extras => Generate Table of Contents**.

I open the Table of Contents text in the Story Editor and select the bold font for the lines of text I wish to stand out from the rest of the elements listed.

I added the title "Table of Contents" and changed the font to Times New Roman Bold and the font size to 12 and save and close, if I have not created a Paragraph Style for the TOC. I also give the table of contents one last check to make sure the dot filler is working on every line, and that the page numbers line up down the right hand side of the page.

If you find any errors, you can adjust the position of the tab on the ruler in the TOC Style window, then delete the TOC text and generate the TOC again. Remember, you can alter your Fixed Linespacing if your TOC list flows onto the next page text field or if there is a large blank space at the bottom of the TOC page.

Creating an Index at the back of a non-fiction book or a list of characters for a fiction book is the same process as creating the Table of Contents.

For this book, I added two pages at the end of the book and placed two text frames on a right side page, leaving a gap between them. I linked the two text frames so the text would flow into the second column (text frame) after it filled the first text frame.

I also created a Paragraph Style called Index to include the tab where the page number lines up and the size of the font is smaller than the TOC font size. I also selected **Dot** in the **Fill Char:** field.

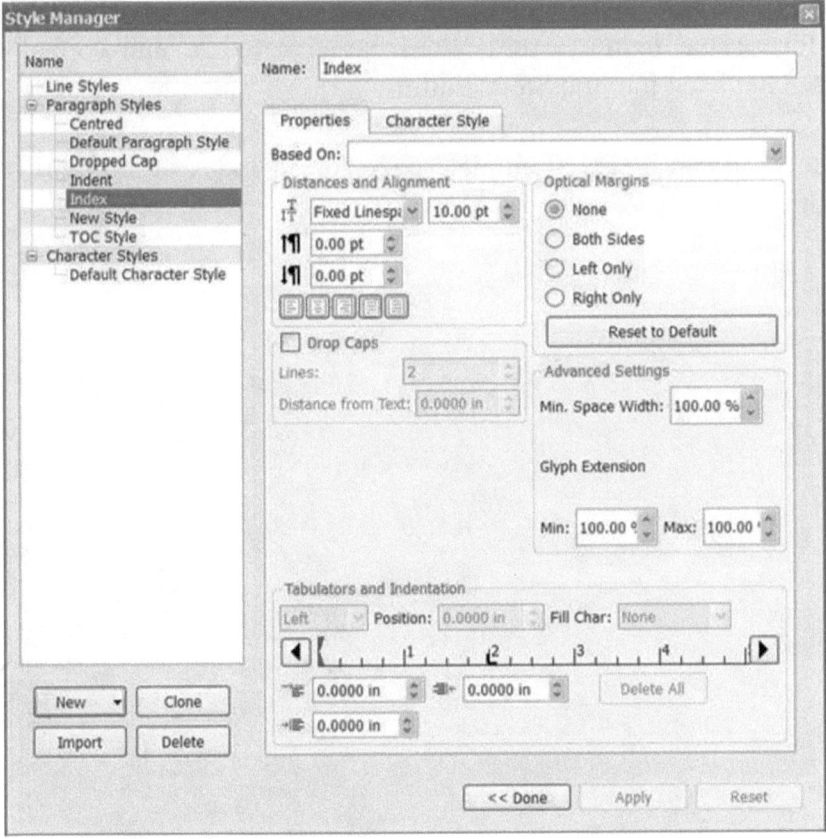

I went through each page from the start to the end of the book, selecting the page for each word I wanted included in the list. I right clicked the selected page text frame and selected **Attributes** and added the word, the same as for the TOC.

When I finish adding the attributes I save the document before I select the index frame and generate the Index.

At the same time the TOC regenerated. So, I had to reselect the bold font for the TOC.

The index built the list with the required words and page numbers, but it was in order of the pages.

To sort the list alphabetically, I copied the index list in the Story Editor, pasted it into a new Word page, sorted it, and copied the sorted list back into the Story Editor.

Note: You can create a template page for an Index and import it to future layout files.

Compiling into PDF

Next I make a PDF file, almost ready to upload to CreateSpace.

I always do one last check of the page numbering sections before compiling the PDF interior file, because I could have added more pages or deleted pages as I worked through adjusting the widows and orphans and any added front or back matter. Remember, to change each section page numbering, click **File => Document Setup, Sections**.

Select the **File => Export** menu item and click on **Save as PDF. . .** to open the **Preflight Verifier** window.

Every template and page is listed under **Items**.

Scan the whole list looking for any items that do not have a green check (tick) displayed beside the item.

When you locate a **red triangle with an exclamation mark in it**, it means there is a problem item in the file, so you have to locate the item and fix or delete it.

I found they were usually free floating text frames and easy to fix the problem. Double click on the item and it will select and display the problem item in the Scribus window. Delete it.

Click the **Check again** button at the bottom of the Preflight Verifier window and confirm all the errors have been removed.

If not, double click on the listed items and remove them, and check again until you receive the message **Document No Problems found**. Click the **OK** button and the **Save as PDF** window opens.

Enter a **Output to File:** path for the PDF file. I leave the file name the same as the Scribus file name, but you may want to give the PDF file a different name.

I leave most of the settings as they are, but change **Compatibility: to PDF 1.3 (Acrobat 4)**, if it displays a later version, and embed all the fonts.

I click the **Save** button to generate the PDF file.

You can open the PDF file in Adobe Reader and confirm all settings are correct. If not, make the changes in the Scribus **Story Editor**, and recompile the PDF file.

Exercise:

1. Check your page numbering is correct.
2. Compile your PDF file.
3. If there are Preflight Vector errors, remove them, and Check again.
4. When you receive the message **Document No Problems found**, click **OK**.
5. Select the path for the PDF file and any other configuration changes you need, and create the PDF file.
6. Open the PDF file in Adobe Reader and check for layout errors.
7. Fix any adjustments you require in Scribus and compile the PDF file again.

You have now completed the interior layout for your POD book. The only future change you need is to add the ISBN number to the Front Matter Copyright page when CreateSpace assigns you the number.

Adding ISBN to Front Matter

When your ISBN number is received from CreateSpace or another POD company, you need to open the Scribus file and copy and paste the ISBN into the Copyright page marker, removing the text "13 digit number goes here".

Next recompile as PDF and save to the same file name so there is no confusion as to which is the current file.

Now you upload to CreateSpace.

Exercise:

1. Open your final draft interior book file in Scribus, not your PDF file.
2. Add your ISBN number to your Copyright page.
3. Confirm you removed the **"13 digit number goes here"** marker.
4. Save the file to the same Scribus named file so there is no confusion as to the version.
5. Export to PDF and save to the same PDF file name you used previously.
6. You now have both a Scribus file and a PDF file with the allocated ISBN number in the Copyright page.
7. You are now ready to upload your PDF file to CreateSpace.

Next we create a cover for the book.

Creating Book Covers

Create template

First, I calculate the measurements of the cover.

Remember, my example will be a 6" x 9" Black and White book with 152 pages. I need to include Front Matter (approximately 8 pages) and Back Matter (About the Author, Sample of next book, and list of available books and any links so another 8 - 10 pages) totalling 170 pages.

You need to return to the start of this book and confirm your book size and the total number of pages, including Front and Back Matter.

My front cover will be 6" x 9" plus bleed. I will be using .25" bleed on top, bottom and right side. So, my measurements for the front are 6.00" x 9.00". The same measurements for the back.

The spine is book height x width of spine which is calculated by number of pages X thickness of paper.

My spine width will be calculated as 170 pages x 0.0025 (for cream paper) and height will be 9.0" so the spine measurements are 0.425" x 9.0".

Back Cover   **Spine**   **Front Cover**
6.0" x 9.0"   0.425" x 9.0"   6.0" x 9.0"

Note:

You can check with CreateSpace in case of recent changes to any measurements at createspace.com in the Products/Book/CoverPDF page but at the time of writing this, CreateSpace advises the width of the spine is calculated with the following measurements.

For black and white-interior books:
White paper: multiply page count by **0.002252**
Cream paper: multiply page count by **0.0025**

For color-interior books:
Multiply page count by **0.002347**

Minimum Cover Width:
Bleed + Back Cover Trim Size + Spine Width + Front Cover Trim Size + Bleed

Example calculation:
For 6" x 9" cover with 60 B&W pages on white paper:
0.125" + 6" + 0.135" + 6" + .125" = 12.385"

Minimum Cover Height:
Bleed + Book Height Trim Size + Bleed

Example calculation:
6" x 9": 0.125" + 9" + .125" = 9.25"

Exercise:

1. Calculate the size of the front and back cover, including the bleed area.
2. Calculate the thickness of spine by multiplying number of pages (including front and back matter) x .0025 (cream paper) or .002252 (white paper) or .002347 (colour interior).

Create template with calculated measurements

Open Scribus and select **File => New** and the New Document window opens.

Select **Inches** as the measurement in **Default Unit:**

You can use Single page or 3-Fold but I select the **Single Page** icon. The width will be the sum of the Back, Spine and Front pages width (6.0 + 0.425 + 6.0 totalling 12.425"). The height remains 9.0". I enter width 12.4250" and height 9.0000".

I select **Landscape Orientation**.

Next I click on the **Bleeds** Tab and enter 0.2500" in **Inside**. I confirm the **chain icon** to the right of the Bleeds area is not broken. If it is, I click on it to join the chain links, and the other three fields will change to 0.2500".

I click on the **Margin Guides** tab and enter 0.2500" in **Left**. I confirm the **chain icon** to the right of the Margin Guides area is not broken. If it is, I click on it to join the chain links, and the other three fields will change to 0.2500".

I leave the rest of the settings as they are and click OK.

The New Document window closes, and the new page appears in the main Scribus window. I make sure the new page is selected, and click on the menu item **Page => Manage Guides** to open the **Guide Manager** window.

Under the Verticals (in) area of the Guide Manager window, I click the **Add** button and enter 6.0000 to make a guide for the left side of the spine. I click the **Add** button again and enter 6.4250" to make a guide for the right of the spine.

I add two more guides, entering 6.0625 and 6.3625 for guides for adding text to the spine because I **must** leave **.0625"** space either side of the spine free to allow CreateSpace to adjust when printing.

These guides will help me align the text frames on the spine.

I click the **Apply to All Pages** button to close the Guides Manager window.

I am now ready to add the image and text frames to the cover layout.

Exercise:

1. Create your template using your calculated measurements in the previous exercise.
2. Add two guides for your spine width, and two guides .0625" inside your right and left spine guides.
3. Save your template.

Insert Image

How you design your cover is up to you.

Your choices are:
• One image covering front, spine and back.
• Front cover image only with Spine and Back cover plain colour
• Or front and back covers both the same image, and a plain colour for the spine

For my fiction novels, I use one image covering the front, spine and back, making sure the image is 300 DPI.

I use the - or + magnifying glasses at the bottom of the main Scribus window to make the whole cover visible in the main Scribus window.

Then I go to the **Insert** menu item and select **Insert Image Frame**. The mouse pointer changes to a + sign with an icon of an image.

I move the mouse pointer to the top left corner of the back cover area on the template and while holding down the left mouse button, I drag the mouse pointer down and across the page to the bottom right corner of the front template, then release the mouse.

If the image is not exact, I move the mouse pointer to the red squares in the middle of each side, or the corner red squares until the mouse pointer changes to arrows and drag the frame to the correct size. I right click the mouse inside the image frame and select **Get Image** from the drop down menu list.

I navigate to the correct path of the image file in the **Open** window and once selected, I click the **OK** button.

I right click the mouse on the imported image and select **Adjust Image to Frame** from the drop down menu list.

If the image still does not cover the whole cover template including the bleed area, then I place the mouse pointer on the corner red square and drag the image down and out until it does cover the entire template area, even if the image frame extends below the actual template frame.

I right click on the image and select **Properties** from the drop down menu. I click on the **Colours** tab and set **Opacity** to 50% so I can see the guide lines and bleed lines through the picture. I then drag the image frame left or right until I am satisfied the image is the best fit for the cover taking into account what part of the image is displayed on the spine.

I close the **Properties** box, right click on the image and select **Size is Locked** so the image is not accidentally moved while I add and arrange the text frames.

Exercise:

1. Click the **Zoom Out (-)** or **Zoom In (+)** Magnifying Glass icons at the bottom of the Scribus main window so you can see the whole cover template.
2. Add an **Image Frame**.
3. Add your image.
4. Bring the **Opacity** down to 50% so you can confirm the image covers the whole template. You can leave the opacity at 50% until after you add your text frames and text because you will use your guides for aligning the text frames.
5. Lock the image to your selected correct size.
6. Save the file.

Front Cover Text

At the least, you need a Title and Author Text Frame on the Front cover. Study the published books in the genre you write and work out if you need more than you Book Title and Your Author Name and notice the placement of each text frame on covers you like.

I add Title, Author, and other information such as series number.

I click **Insert, Insert Text Frame** and place it across the top of the Front Cover, making sure to keep the edges of the text frame inside the blue margin on the top and right sides.

I also make sure I keep the left edge the same distance from the right spine guide as the outer edge, .25". If I am not sure, I add another guide .25" to the right of the right spine guide.

I **right click** the mouse while the pointer is in the text frame and select **Edit Text** to open the Story Editor and enter the title of my novel. Then I make sure I have selected the text, then select the font and size and click **Update Text Frame and Exit** icon to save the text and settings. I repeat opening the Story Editor until I am happy with the height and width of the title text.

I repeat the above steps to add a Text Frame for my Author Name, and any other information I require on the front of my cover.

That is how easy it is to add the text to the front cover.

Exercise:

1. Add a guide to the left side of the front cover equal to the width of your page margins.
2. Add a text frame for the title of your story and arrange on the front cover.

3. Add the text for the title and adjust the justification, font, size, height and width.

4. Repeat for your Author Name.

5. Save the file.

Spine Text

I place the Title, Author, Publisher Icon and Genre on the spine.

Again, I suggest you check other published books in your genre to see what text they include on the spine.

I add four **text frames**, and while the text frames are still horizontal, I add the text and adjust the font family, width and height of the text, and select the colour, and save and exit the Story Editor.

Then I change the horizontal fields to vertical for Title and Author Name. I select each text frame in turn, right click, and open the **Properties** window. I select the **XYZ tab** and change the value for **Rotation** to **270.0 °**

Take note of the cover spine text direction in the genre published books you studied. The published spines I studied all flow the text fields of Author and Title on the spine from top to bottom, not from bottom to top, hence the rotation to 270 degrees. If you need your text to flow from the bottom to the top of the spine, then you would select 90 degrees rotation.

I can see other places where I could use the rotation of 90 degrees, such as the front or rear cover text on a non-fiction cover.

The genre and publisher icon I keep horizontal and adjust the size of the font until it fits. I found that if I place "Science" and "Fiction" over two lines and adjust the font size until it fits within the guides at the sides of the spine it is still readable by the book store staff, helping them place the title in the correct genre shelves.

I sometimes select **Line Spacing** under **Text, First Line Offset** tabs, if the text in the text frame does not line up correctly, but mostly, I move the **Text Frame** or alter the font size until the text is displayed correctly inside the spine guides.

I move the text frame to the correct position on the spine and repeat for the two other text frames. The publisher icon I leave horizontal. I move it to the correct position on the spine, and adjust until the publisher icon is inside the spine margins.

The spine is done for now.

Exercise:

1. If you have not already added the guides for your spine, do so now.
2. If your front cover image does not flow across your spine, you need to add an image frame and image to your spine. You may use a single colour instead of an image, but pick a colour that allows the text to be clearly read on a book shelf. Again, study other published books in your chosen genre for comparison.
3. Add your text frames and enter your book title, author name, genre and publisher icon or text.
4. Select the correct font family, size, with width and height adjustments.
5. Change your rotation to flow from the top to bottom of spine.
6. Move each text frame to the correct position on the spine, keeping within the guides.
7. Make any minor adjustments, to colour, height or width of text.
8. When you are satisfied with the placement of the text frames save your file.

Back Cover Text

Again, study the back cover in the genre you write.

I studied a lot of Science Fiction covers, and the main thing I noticed is they all differ in length of blurb, publisher information and the placement of each text frame.

I am not teaching how to write blurbs, only how to use Scribus to create professional covers and interiors. There are many good courses on the internet, from free to small fee, where you can learn how to write good blurbs.

I write my blurb for my ebook, and use the same blurb, with minor changes for the back cover of my POD books.

First, I check the image already added does cover the bleed areas on the back cover, just like the front and spine. I dealt with that step above under front cover heading.

If you are adding an image that is different to the front cover image, then add your image frame and confirm it covers all the bleed areas on the back cover.

I use a text frame for the Blurb and Publisher Data including the cover image copyright.

I also place an empty text or image frame as per CreateSpace requirements until I am satisfied with the placement of the other frames.

CreateSpace requires a 2" x 1.2" box in the lower right hand corner of the back cover. You can check the CreateSpace web link, in case they makes changes to the size of their barcode space since this book was published, at createspace.com in the Products/Book/CoverPDF page.

I make my barcode text or image frame 2.5" x 1.7" which includes a 1/4" margin around the edge, so I know I can place the bottom right corner of the frame against the bottom right corner of the back cover and right side of the barcode frame against the spine guide. This still allows a 1/4" space around the barcode when it is added to the back cover.

Once the barcode frame is placed, I then enlarge the publisher details and blurb frames, making sure neither cross into the barcode area.

I add the text to both text frames and spend a few minutes adjusting the colour and font size until it is readable from a distance.

I sometimes place an image frame behind the blurb and publisher data text frames to lower or dim the cover image enough for the text to be clearly read.

I do this by selecting the blank image frame, right clicking the mouse to select Level from the drop down menu. I send the image frame behind the text frame but in front of the first image frame. Then I select Properties from the drop down list and under Colours I select a pale colour and set the opacity between 50 - 70%,

I study the back cover, making sure the text is clearly read over the second image frame, keeping in mind if a reader picks up my book from a shelf, they only spend seconds reading the back cover. If the font is too small they will return the book to the shelf and select another book.

When I am finally satisfied with the placement and readability of the text, I save the file.

Exercise:

1. If your front cover image does not carry across your spine and

back cover, you need to add an **image frame** and **image** to your back cover.

2. Add your **image frame** for the barcode, making sure it is larger than the area CreateSpace requires.

3. Add your blurb and publisher **text frames**.

4. Add your text to the text frames in the Story Editor.

5. Adjust the font size, width and height.

6. Confirm that the text in the blurb and publisher data frames can be read.

7. If not, add a second image frame, and select a pale colour.

8. Move the image frame one level down, so it is behind the text frame.

9. Again, check that the text can be clearly read.

10. When satisfied with the layout, save the file.

You have now created a professional cover for your Print on Demand book.

Next you will save the completed file as a PDF.

Saving Your Cover File

The only difference between generating a PDF cover file and a PDF interior file is to make sure that the bleeds are included in the generated PDF file.

File, Export => Save as PDF to open the **Preflight Verifier** window. Look for errors.

I always check for **Object has Transparency** errors. If it relates to the cover image, I know I have a habit of not adjusting it after I complete changes to the text frames, so I need to change it back to **100%**.

To do that, I right click on the cover image and select **Properties**. Under the **Colours** tab I change the **Opacity** to **100%** and close the Properties window.

I then close the **Preflight Verifier** and check that all the text is still clearly read. If not, I make adjustments. If I can not make more adjustments, I may decide to drop the Opacity a little lower than 100%, such as 90 or 80%.

Once I am satisfied with the change I again click **File, Export => Save as PDF** and ignore the error message Object has transparency for the cover image.

I also ignore the error message Object has transparency if it refers to a second image that helps lower the cover image so the text can be more easily read.

If there are still other fields with error messages, either remove the excess fields, or fix the frame so that the error messages disappear when you click the **Check Again** button, and finally I click the **Ignore Errors** button to open the **Save as PDF** window.

I check the **Output to File:** path for the pdf file. I leave the file name the same as the Scribus file name, but you may want to give the PDF file a different name.

I click the Ignore Errors button to open the Save as PDF window.

I leave most of the settings as they are, but change **Compatibility: to PDF 1.3 (Acrobat 4)**, if it displays a later version, and embed all the fonts.

Under the **Viewer** tab I confirm **Document Layout** has **Single Page** selected.

Under the **Pre-Press** tab I confirm there is a **check** mark in **Use Document Bleeds**.

That is all the changes needed. I click the **Save** button to generate the PDF file.

I now have both a profession cover and interior layout file ready to upload to CreateSpace created in Scribus that has no visible differences to creating the same files in InDesign.

Exercise:

1. Save your file as a PDF by clicking **File, Export => Save as PDF** to open the **Preflight Verifier** window.
2. Check for any errors and fix then click the **Check Again** button to confirm the errors have been fixed or click the **Ignore Errors** button to open the **Save as PDF** window.
3. Confirm the correct file path and name in the Save as PDF window.
4. Change the Compatibility field to **PDF 1.3 (Acrobat 4)**, end embed the fonts.
5. Change the **Document Layout** has **Single Page** is selected in the Viewer tab.

6. Under the **Pre-Press** tab select **Use Document Bleeds**.
7. Click the **Save** button.

Congratulations. You now have profession cover and interior layout files for your fiction novel ready to upload to CreateSpace that was created in Scribus and has no visible differences to creating the same files in InDesign.

You also have a template that you can use again and again, only changing the image and text fields for each new book.

And, you now have the knowledge to create different sized templates for different works, such as novels, novellas, and collections of short stories.

Final Information

Further Applications

Using the same principles of adding image frames and linking and unlinking text frames, you can create Middle Grade Books and Non Fiction Books with pictures scattered throughout.

You can create marketing material such as bookmarks, flyers, posters and news letters utilising multiple columns, graphics, and many different font shapes and sizes.

Preferences

Click **File => Preferences** to open the Preferences window.

Under the **External Tools** icon you can add external executable programs, such as an Image Processing Tool. I have GIMP installed on my computer, and when I installed Scribus it automatically opened GIMP.

I prefer to use Adobe Photoshop for editing my images, so I added the full path to Adobe Photoshop in my computer and removed the full path to GIMP.

Now, I can right click the mouse on any image and select **Edit Image** to open Adobe Photoshop. I locate the image, make changes, and return to Scribus, update the image and repeat if further changes are needed.

I also changed the Web Browser listed in Scribus to Chrome, by adding the full path to Chrome in my computer.

Remember to click the **Apply** button to save the settings.

Under the **Hyphenator** icon the default settings are off.

If you wish to turn on **Hyphenation Suggestions** or **Hyphenate Text Automatically During Typing**, select the settings in the Hyphenator window.

Click the **Apply** button to save the settings.

The **Keyboard Shortcuts** Icon allows you to add your own shortcuts to some of the actions in Scribus.

If you wish to add shortcuts, you select the action in the list, click the **User Defined Key** radio button, and add your shortcut in the **Set Key** field. Make sure your new key is not already assigned to another action in the list.

There are more areas to change the settings in Preference, but until I learn what changes result from altering the settings, I will not make changes.

Properties

Once I complete all layout pages, I take another look from start to finish, of the first and last lines of each page. I find that because of spacing between paragraphs or headings that are a different font, some pages have jaggered first and last lines as compared to the page beside them.

Properties holds the solution.

In **Properties => Text => First Line Offset**, a list of three properties help to line up the first and last lines across pages.

Maximum Ascent sets the height of the first line of the text frame to use the tallest height of the included characters.

In the below image, the first line in the left page is set higher than the first line in the right page with the First Line Offset set to Maximum Ascent in the Properties window.

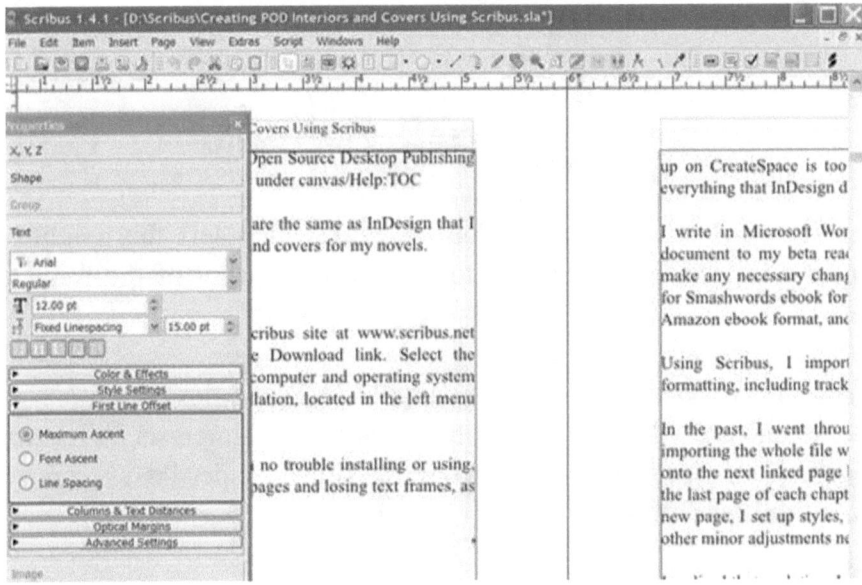

Line Spacing sets the height of the first line of the text frame to use the specified line height.

I select the text frame, open **Properties => Text => First Line Offset** window to change the Offset setting to **Line Spacing**, confirm the first line now lines up across the two page spread and save the file. The next image shows the first line in the left page moved down slightly, to line up with the first line in the right page text frame.

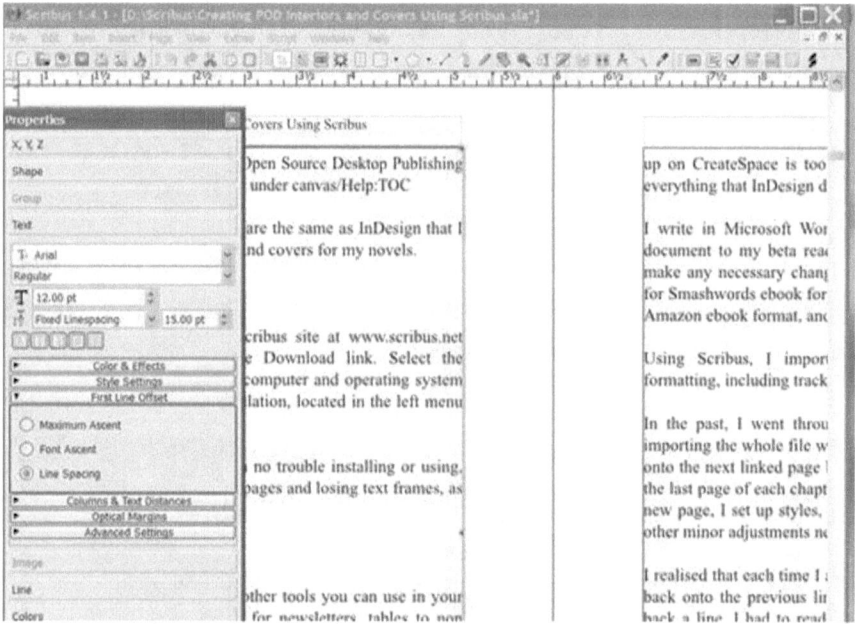

The third offset selection is **Font Ascent** which sets the height of the first line of the text frame to use the full ascent of the fonts in use.

There are many other settings available in Properties, but the ones mentioned are used the most in the layout of interiors of fiction books. I will leave you to discover the other properties as you get more familiar with the software program.

References

Scribus Website:
www.scribus.net

Scribus Help Documentation:
wiki.scribus.net/canvas/Help:TOC

Scribus Program Files for Download:
www.scribus.net/canvas/Scribus

Useful site for information on interior layout:
The Book Designer
www.thebookdesigner.com

Suggested Online Workshops:
Book Cover Design and Interior Book Design
Dean Wesley Smith
www.deanwesleysmith.com

About the Author

D. J. Mills had a career as a Software Engineer, writing programs for businesses, in both the private and public sectors in Australia.

When the author retired from her computer programming career, she started a new career in publishing. She is still learning all facets of publishing, including professional interior layouts, professional book cover design, and marketing.

Learning is a work in progress, so if you discover easier ways to use Scribus, please share your processes with the author at the below contact details.

If you discover typos or other errors, please contact the publisher at the below link so the errors can be removed.

If this guide was helpful and you wish to spread the word, please take a moment to write a review on the site where you purchased the book.

Thank you.

Tift Publishing
www.tiftpublishing.com

Index

Index

www.ingramcontent.com/pod-product-compliance
Lightning Source LLC
Chambersburg PA
CBHW022109170526
45157CB00004B/1548